AXONOMETRICAL PROJECTIONS

OF THE MOST IMPORTANT GEOMETRICAL SURFACES.

DRAWINGS IN DESCRIPTIVE GEOMETRY.

Serving at the same time as a Catalogue of Models executed according to the aforesaid Projections

BY

Ferdinand Engel.

WITH IX PLATES.

EDITION FOR AMERICA.

PREFACE

BY

Dr. Joachimsthal,

PROFESSOR IN THE UNIVERSITY OF HALLE.

NEW YORK,

H. GOEBELER, 343 BROADWAY.

BOSTON: JOSEPH M. WIGHTMAN.—PHILADELPHIA: A. HART.—BALTIMORE: N. HICKMAN.—CINCINNATI: R. ROOT.—MONTREAL: J. ARMOUR.

1855.

PRINTED BY G. B. TEUBNER, 17 ANN ST., N. Y.

PREFACE.

THE collection of models by Mr. ENGEL, and the drawings which he is about to publish as a catalogue of his collection, are so very important for the study of Superior Geometry and Optics that I most willingly yield to the desire of Mr. ENGEL, and ask in a few words, for these interesting publications, the attention of friends of mathematics and of natural philosophy.

It was the model of the wave surface, (Nr. 1 and 2) the first preparation of which presented the main difficulty. For the purpose of giving some notion of the surface with its two sheets and singular points, it was thought sufficient till now to represent its principal sections by means of wires. Mr. ENGEL was the first to succeed in modelling in wood the solid included between the two sheets; this model—properly dissected—permitting an exact inspection of the shape of these sheets. The Jury of the London exhibition, first section, class Xth, (physical, chemical, and other instruments) on account of that model—which is a masterpiece in its way*—bestowed upon Mr. ENGEL the prize-medal. To put the value of that acknowledgment in a proper light I remark, that Sir DAVID BREWSTER was the chairman of the Jury, and Sir JOHN HERSCHEL among its members.

* The first model made by MR. ENGEL is in the possession of Professor PLÜCKER at Bonn, it is mentioned with great praise [but without telling the artist's name] in the: "Einleitung in die höhere Optik von BEER." A second exemplar is in the physical cabinet of the University of Berlin.

The models No. 3—12 represent the five principal classes of surfaces of the second order, with their circular sections, right lines and lines of curvature. For the construction of these lines of curvature Mr. ENGEL, at first, made use only of the projections designed by MONGE. In doing this he found—which I make a point of, in order to give a notion of the accuracy of his graphical constructions—that the rectilinear diagonals of any square formed by arcs of lines of curvature are equal to each other. This is quite new, for aught I know, at least in this shape; we may derive it from the well known theorem of IVORY if we add to it the remark of CHASLES, that a curved line, perpendicularly intersecting a system of confocal surfaces, meets them in corresponding points. The profit which Mr. ENGEL has derived from this circumstance will be mentioned in these explanations.

The models Nr. 13—20 represent cones, combinations of hyperbolical paraboloids, &c.; Nr. 21—27 several helicoids and screws; Nr. 28—30 three rectilinear oblique planes (not belonging to the family of surfaces just mentioned); Nr. 31 and 32 are two developable surfaces; Nr. 35—37 refer to the theory of spherical curves and their polar curves, and so forth.

I should exceed the limits of an advertisement if I were to dwell ever so little on the interesting geometrical problems, which were to be settled before the preparation of the models.

A few more words about the drawings: Though originally intended to serve as an extensive catalogue for the collection of models, they are of considerable use, when used in teaching Superior and Descriptive Geometry. Those who are not very well acquainted with the methods of Descriptive Geometry, will understand the drawings quite as well, Mr. ENGEL'S method of projecting being remarkably similar to Perspective.

Some time since, Mr. ENGEL published two numbers of optical drawings which were most favorably received by Geometers, even in foreign countries. I am quite sure, therefore, that every friend of the higher Mathematics will accept with no little pleasure this new publication of the same author.

F. JOACHIMSTHAL,

PROFESSOR IN THE UNIVERSITY OF HALLE.

CATALOGUE

OF DRAWINGS OF MODELS FOR THE STUDY OF OPTICS AND THE HIGHER BRANCHES OF GEOMETRY,

with the prices of these models made of wood (W.) or of plaster-composition (P.).

The models are to be had by forwarding the amount and 75 cts. for packing, to H. GOEBELER, 343 Broadway, New York.

Besides these models the undersigned has constantly for sale a large number of models and diagrams, made by himself, intended chiefly for instruction in Descriptive as well as in the higher branches of Analytical Geometry.

---

1. Fresnel's Wave Surface of Light in double refracting media, on a wooden stand. The 3 axes a, b, c are to each other as $\sqrt{3} : \sqrt{2} : 1$. $a = 80^{mm}$. Wood $60, Plaster $10.

   This model shews the two sheets of the surface and is decomposable by means of four central sections into two parts in four different ways.

2. Inner part of the Wave Surface convexly represented, of W. $8, P. $3.

2*a*. Fresnel's Wave Surface in which the ratio of the axes is 1,53 : 1,32 : 1. $a = 170^{mm}$. W. $100. P. $20.

2*b*. Inner part of the Wave Surface convexly represented, W. $20. P. $5.

3. Triaxial Ellipsoid, shewing two circular sections, P. $3.

3*a*. The same divided into two parts by a circular central section. W. $10. P. $4.

4. The same with the lines of curvature, P. $10.

5. Hyperboloid of two sheets, shewing two circular sections, on wooden support, P. $8.

6. The same with its lines of curvature, P. $12.

7. Hyperboloid of one sheet, shewing two circular sections and some rectilinear generatrices, P. $8.

8. The same with its lines of curvature, P. $12.

9. Elliptical Paraboloid, shewing two circular sections, P. $4.

10. The same with its lines of curvature, P. $6.

11. Hyperbolical Paraboloid (oblique plane), P. $6.

12. The same with its lines of curvature, P. $8.

13. Right Elliptical Cone, with two circular sections, on wooden support, P. $8.

14. The same with its lines of curvature, P. $10.

15. Double Right Circular Cone, with 3 sections, P. $8.

16. Oblique Circular Cone, with four sections, W. $10.

17. Combination of a Sphere and a Right Elliptical Cone, intersecting each other in two circles, W. $6.

18. Body, enclosed between two squares and four oblique planes, P $5.

19. Body, enclosed between one square and four oblique planes, W. $6.

20. Parallelopiped, divided by an oblique plane into two unequal parts, Zinc $8. P. $6.

   Four Screw-surfaces with their nuts shewing the rectilinear generatrices in different positions.

21. Right Helicoid, P. $6 to 9.

22. Oblique Helicoid, P. $6 to 9.

23. General Helicoid, P. $6 to 9.

24. Developable Helicoid, P. $6 to 9.

25. The same with its lines of curvature, P. $8 to 10.

26. Screw of four grooves, P. $6 to 8.

27. Screw of five grooves, P $6 to 8.

28. Rectilinear oblique surface W. $10 to 12.

29. Another surface of the same kind (elliptical wedge), W. $9. P. $5.

30. A third surface of the same kind, (semi-circular wedge), W. $6. P. $ 3.

31. Developable surface, W. $10. P. $6.

32. Another developable surface, W. $10. P. $6.

33. Serpentine body, P. $6 to 8.

34. Annular body, P. $2.

35. Spherical Curve, with its polar curve, P. $5 to 6.

36. Sphere with four main circles, P. $1 to 2.

37. Spherical Triangle with its symmetrical and polar triangle. W. $8. P. $4.

38. Combination of five Cubes, a crystaline form found sometimes in pyrites, P. $4.

39. Same body, each of the five cubes differently coloured, P. $6 to 8.

40. Four Measuring-scales on wood, intended for the axonometrical method of projection, W. $3.

41. Cube, W. $00.30.

42. Three axis intersecting each other perpendicular, W. $00.30.

For a more detailed description of the surfaces enumerated in this catalogue see the "Explanations."

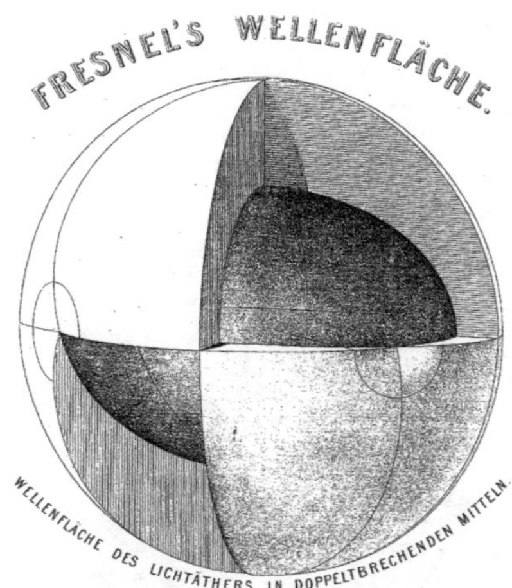

AXONOMETRICAL PROJECTIONS

OF THE MOST IMPORTANT GEOMETRICAL SURFACES

DRAWINGS OF DESCRIPTIVE GEOMETRY

SERVING IN THE SAME TIME AS A CATALOGUE OF MODELS
CARRIED OUT ACCORDING TO THE AFORESAID PROJECTIONS

BY

FERDINAND ENGEL.

WITH IX PLATES.

AXONOMETRISCHE PROJECTIONEN

DER WICHTIGSTEN GEOMETRISCHEN FLÄCHEN

VORLEGEBLÄTTER FÜR BESCHREIBENDE GEOMETRIE

ZUGLEICH ALS CATALOG EINER MODELLSAMMLUNG VON KÖRPERN
DIE NACH DEN VORGENAÑTEN PROJECTIONEN AUSGEFÜHRT WORDEN SIND

VON

FERDINAND ENGEL.

MIT IX FIGURENTAFELN.

PROJECTIONS AXONOMÉTRIQUES

DES SURFACES GÉOMÉTRIQUES LES PLUS IMPORTANTES

MODÈLES DE DESSIN DE GÉOMÉTRIE DESCRIPTIVE

SERVANT EN MÊME TEMPS DE CATALOGUE D'UNE COLLECTION
DE SOLIDES DE GÉOMÉTRIE CONSTRUITS SUR CES PROJECTIONS

PAR

FERDINAND ENGEL.

AVEC IX PLANCHES.

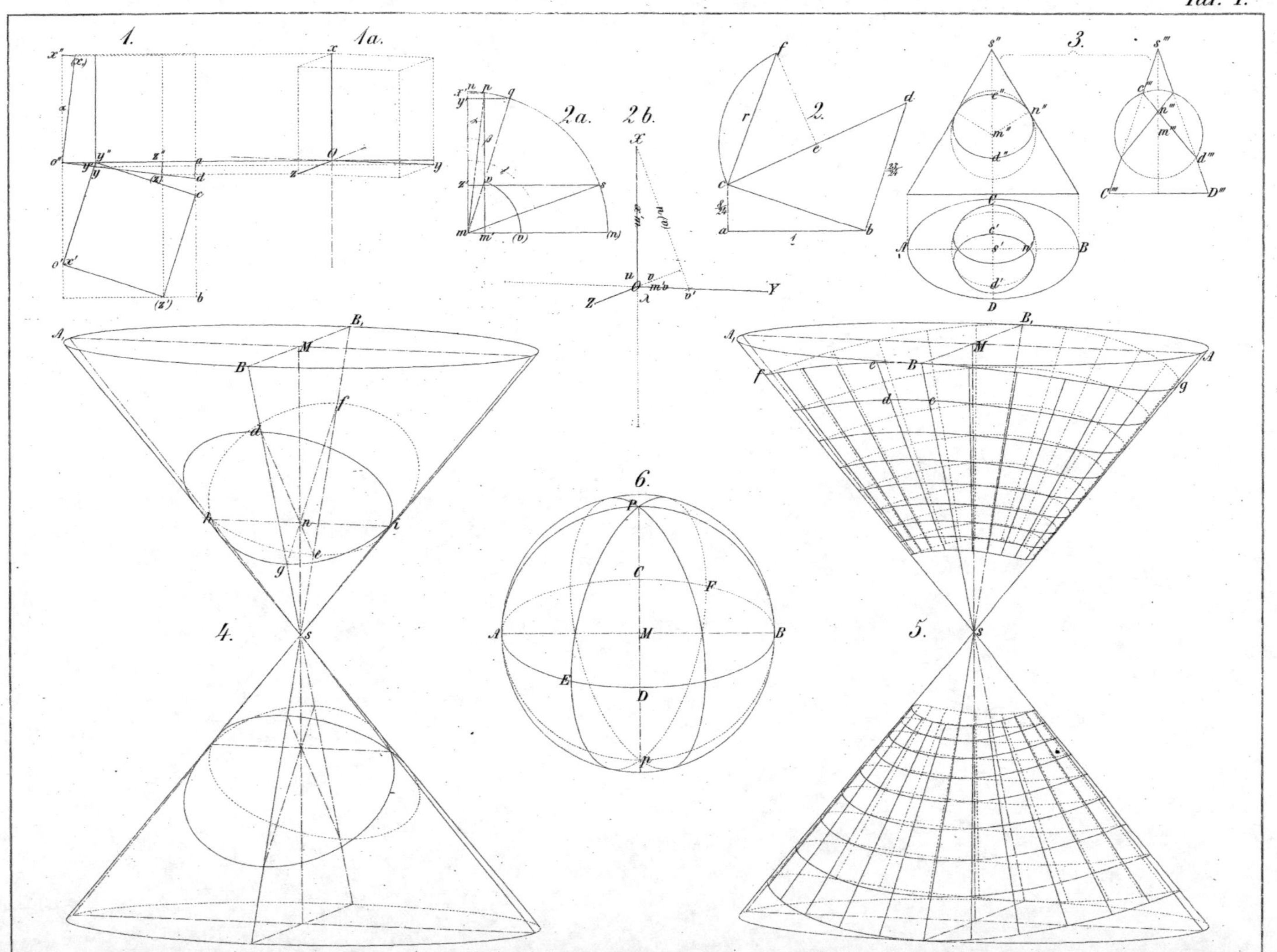
1.
1a.
2a.
2b.
2.
3.
4.
5.
6.
x
y
z
o
X
Y
Z
O
s″
s‴
s
M
A
B
C
D
E
F
P
p

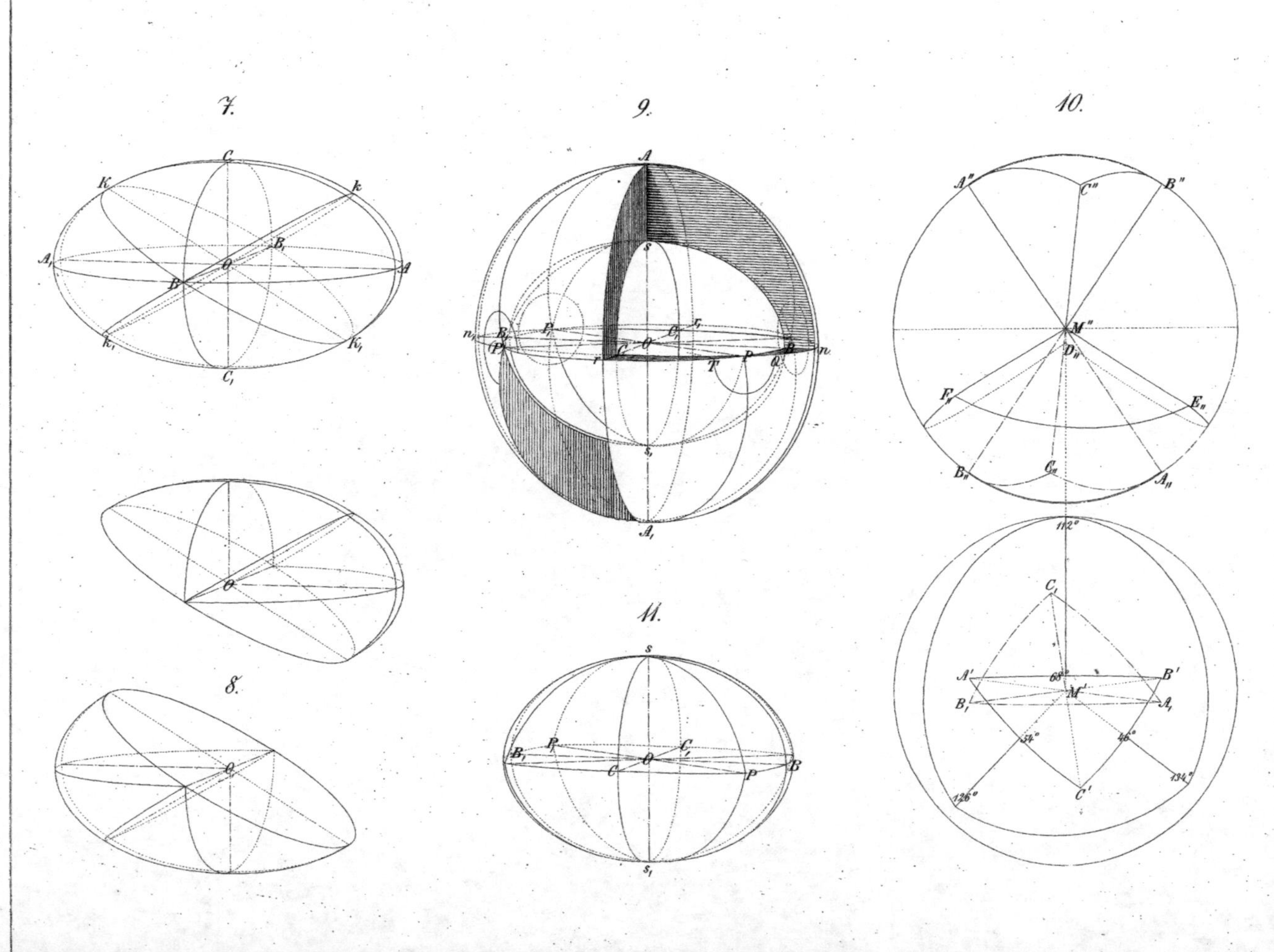

const. u. grav. v. F. Engel.

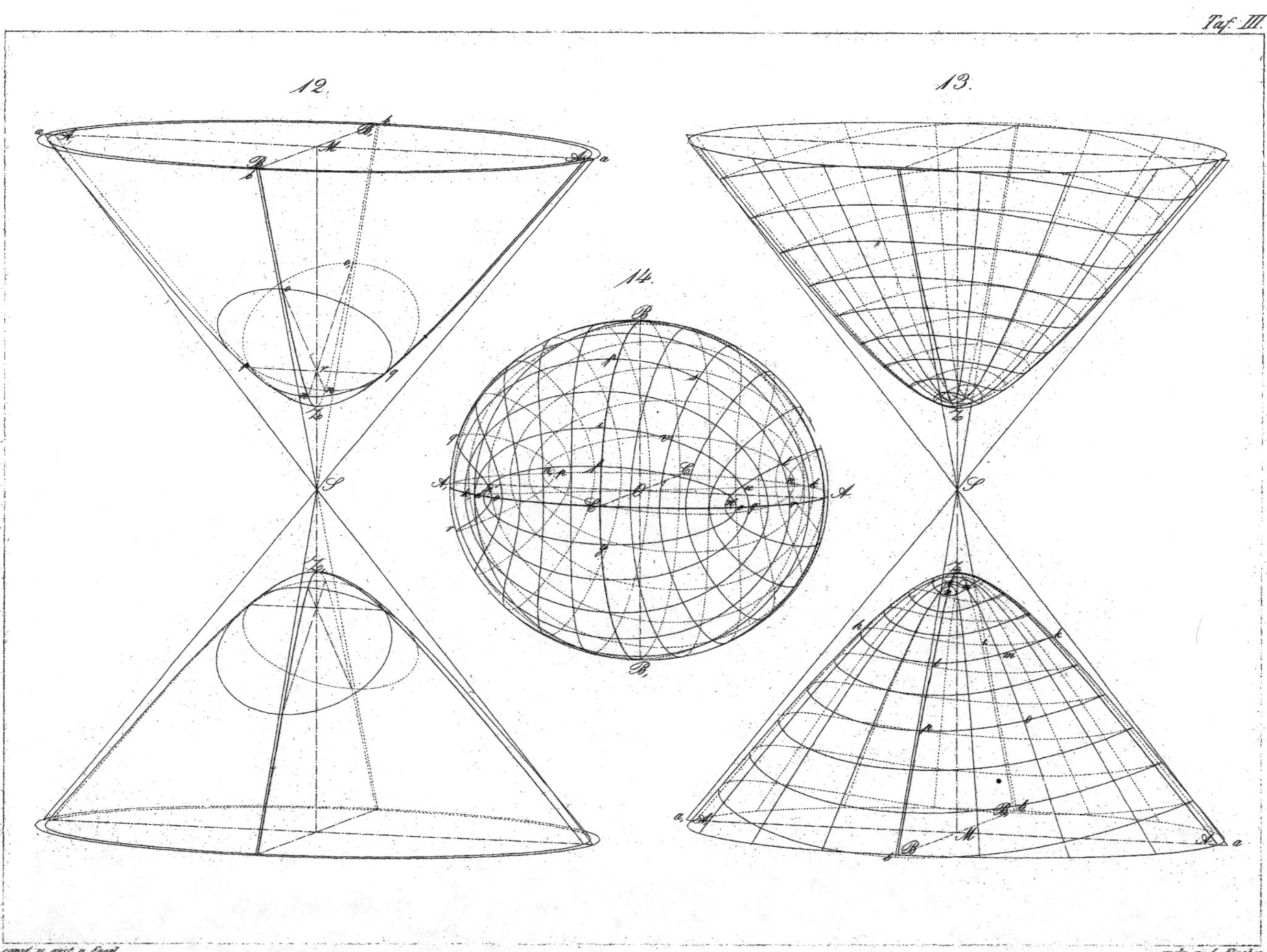
Taf. III.
12.
14.
13.
const. u. gest. v. Engel.
gedr. v. L. Fischer.

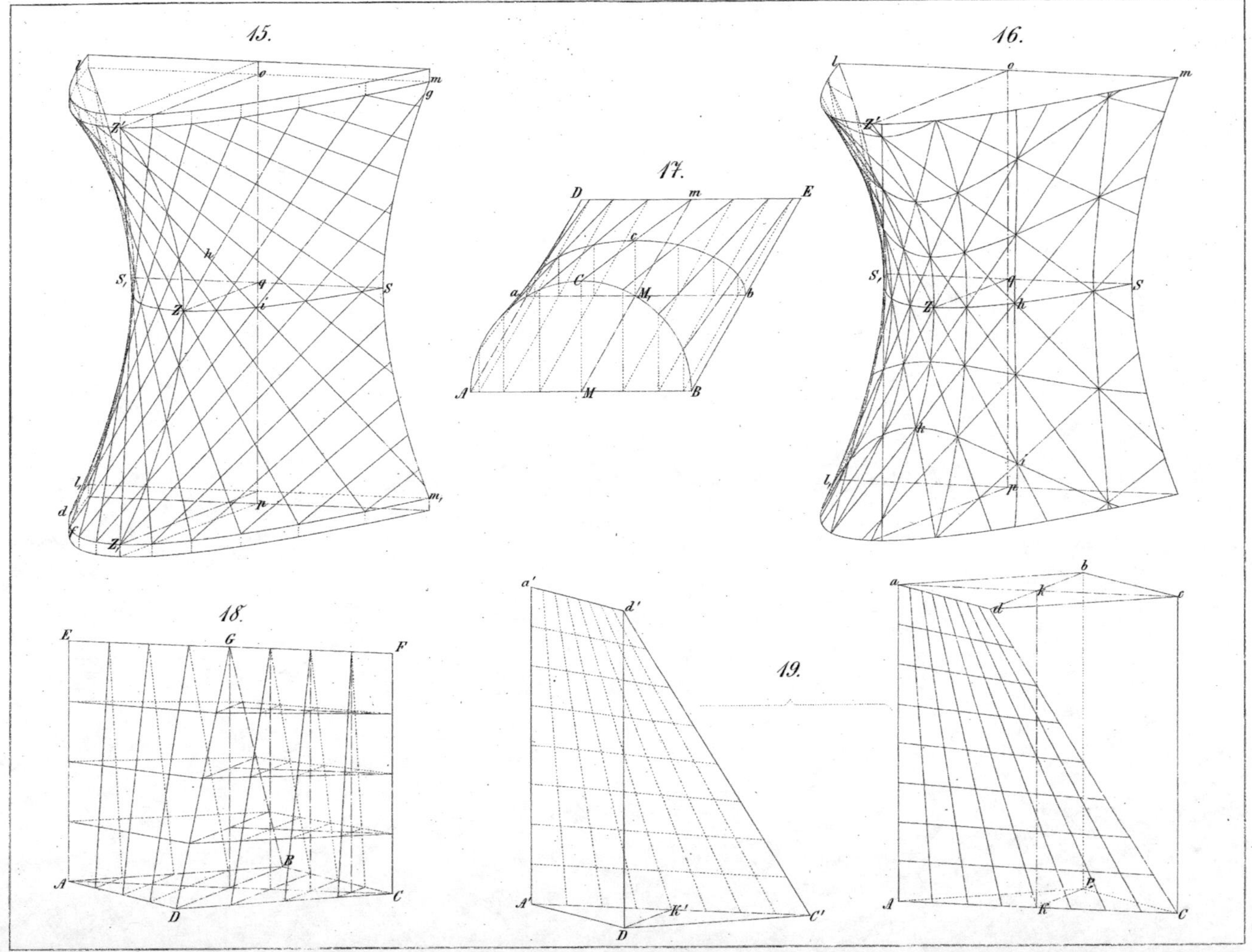
15.
16.
17.
18.
19.
const. u. grav. v. F. Engel.

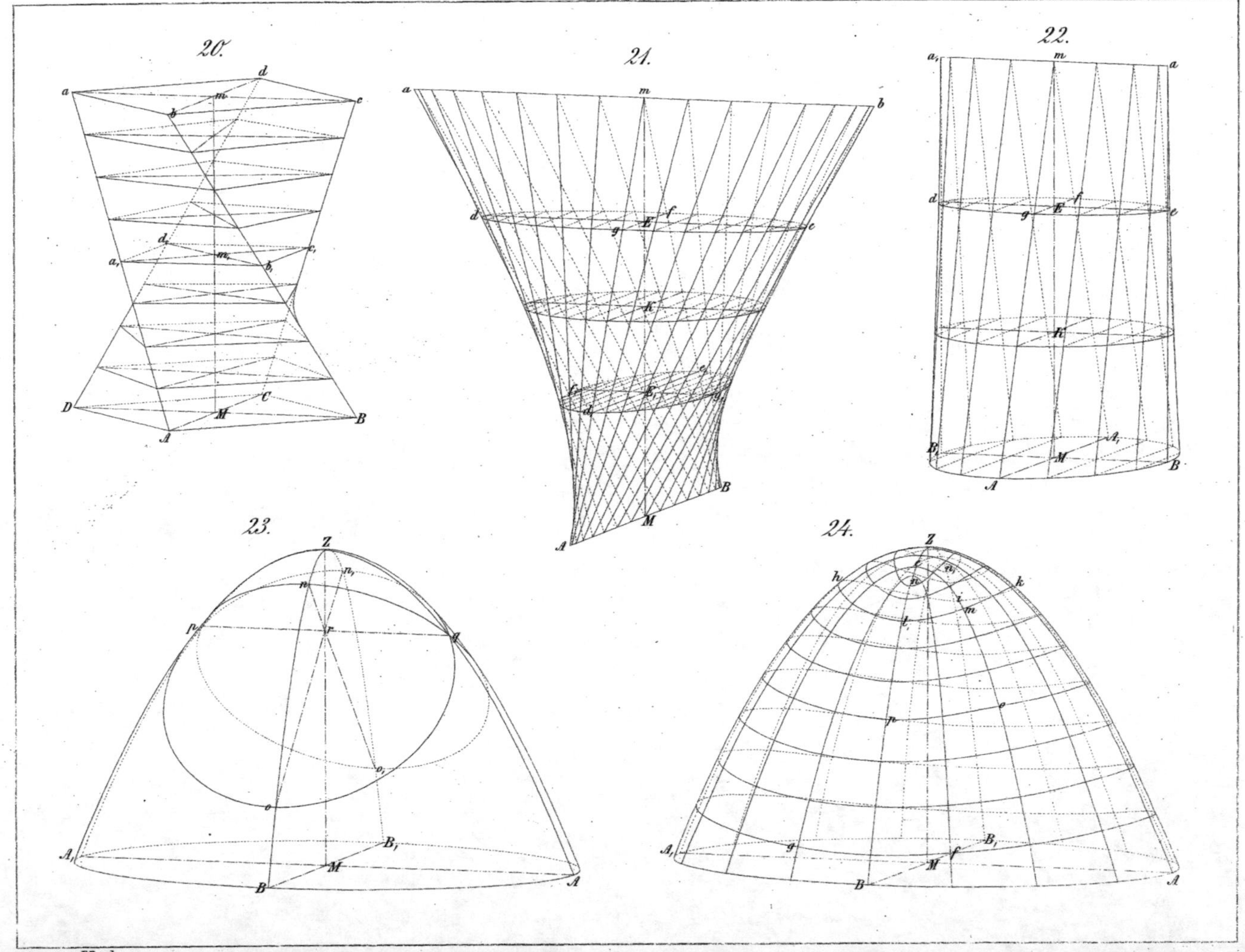

const. u. grav. u. E. Engel.

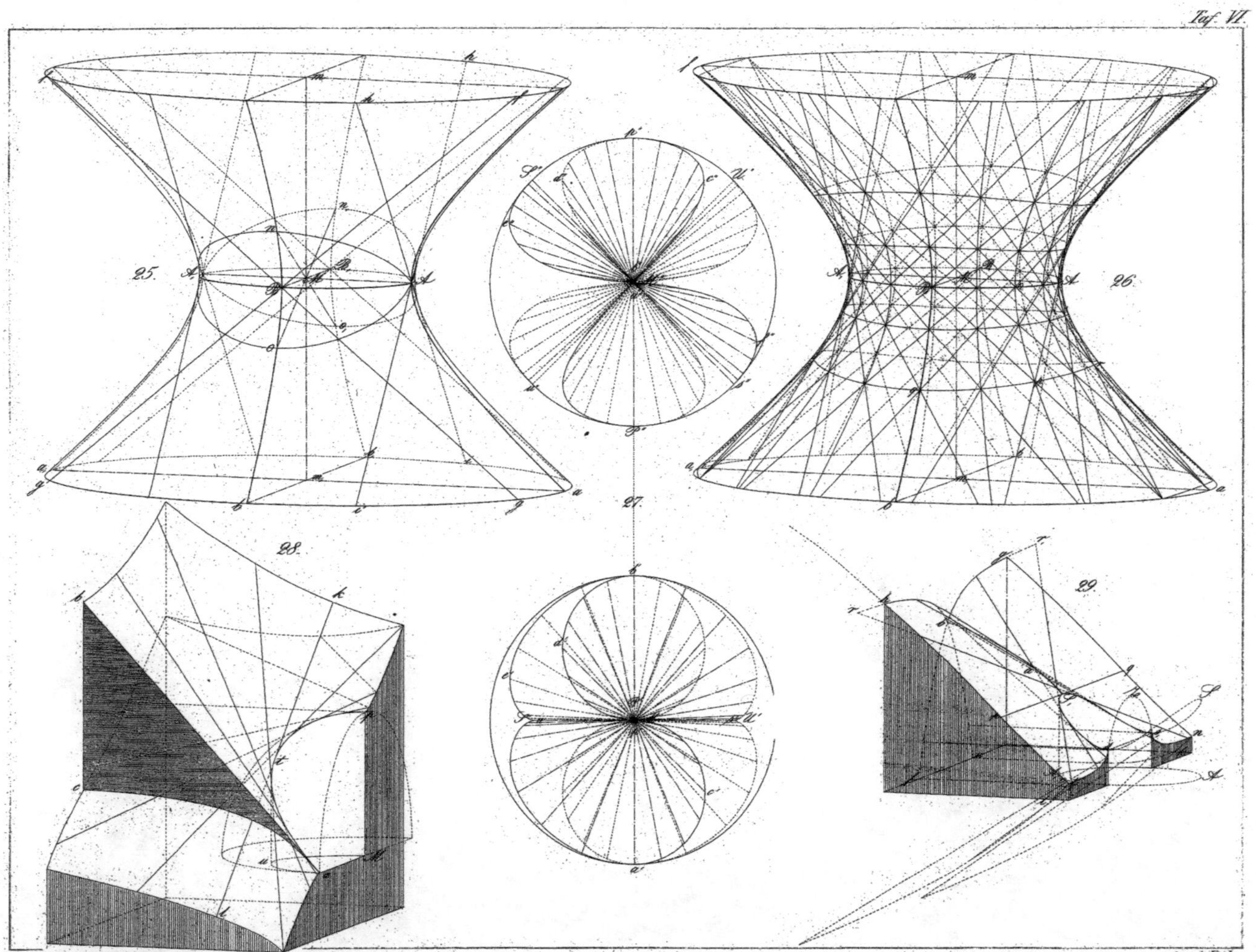

const. u. gest. v. F. Engel.

gedr. v. L. Fischer.

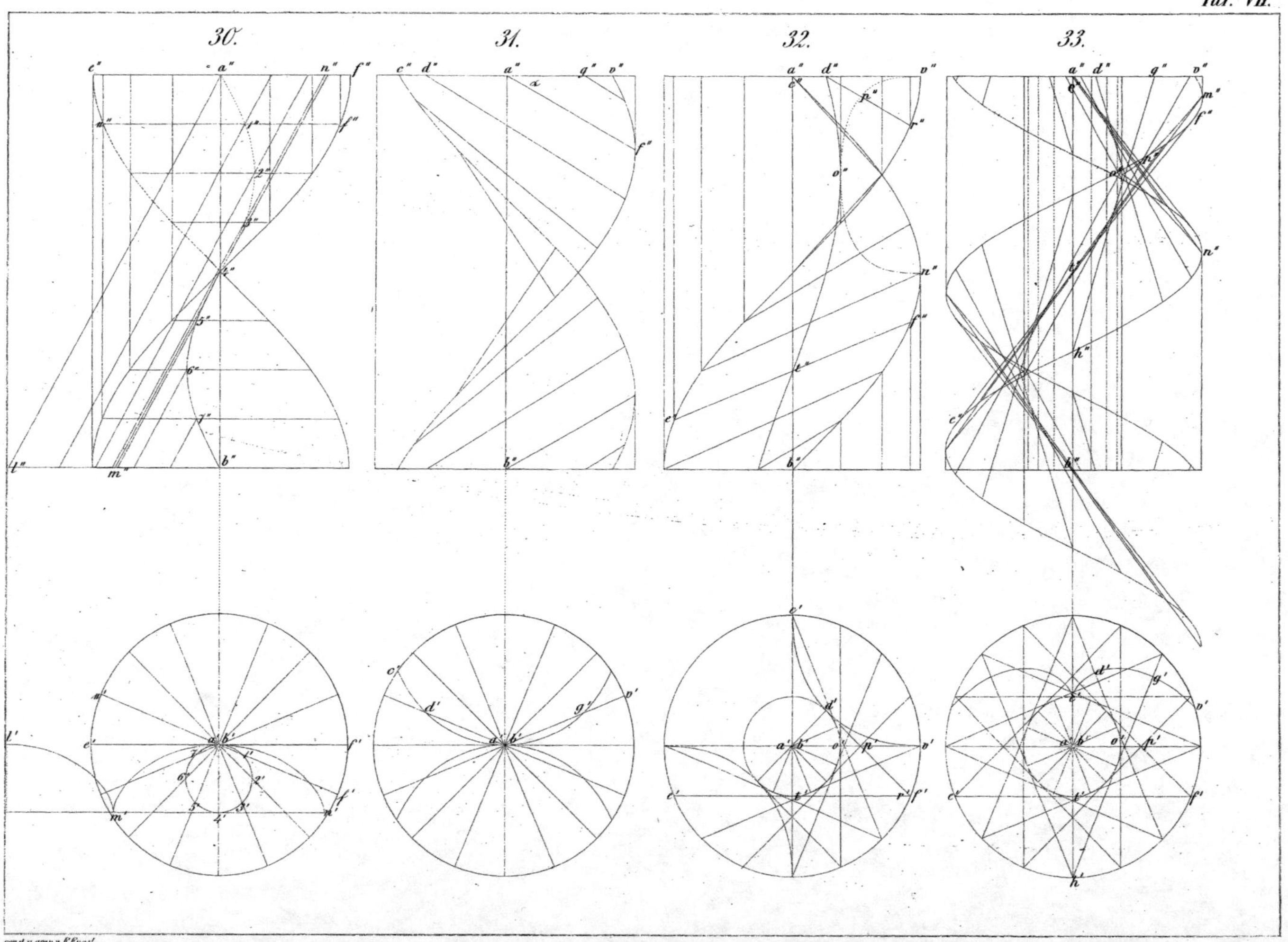

const. u. grav. v. F. Engel.

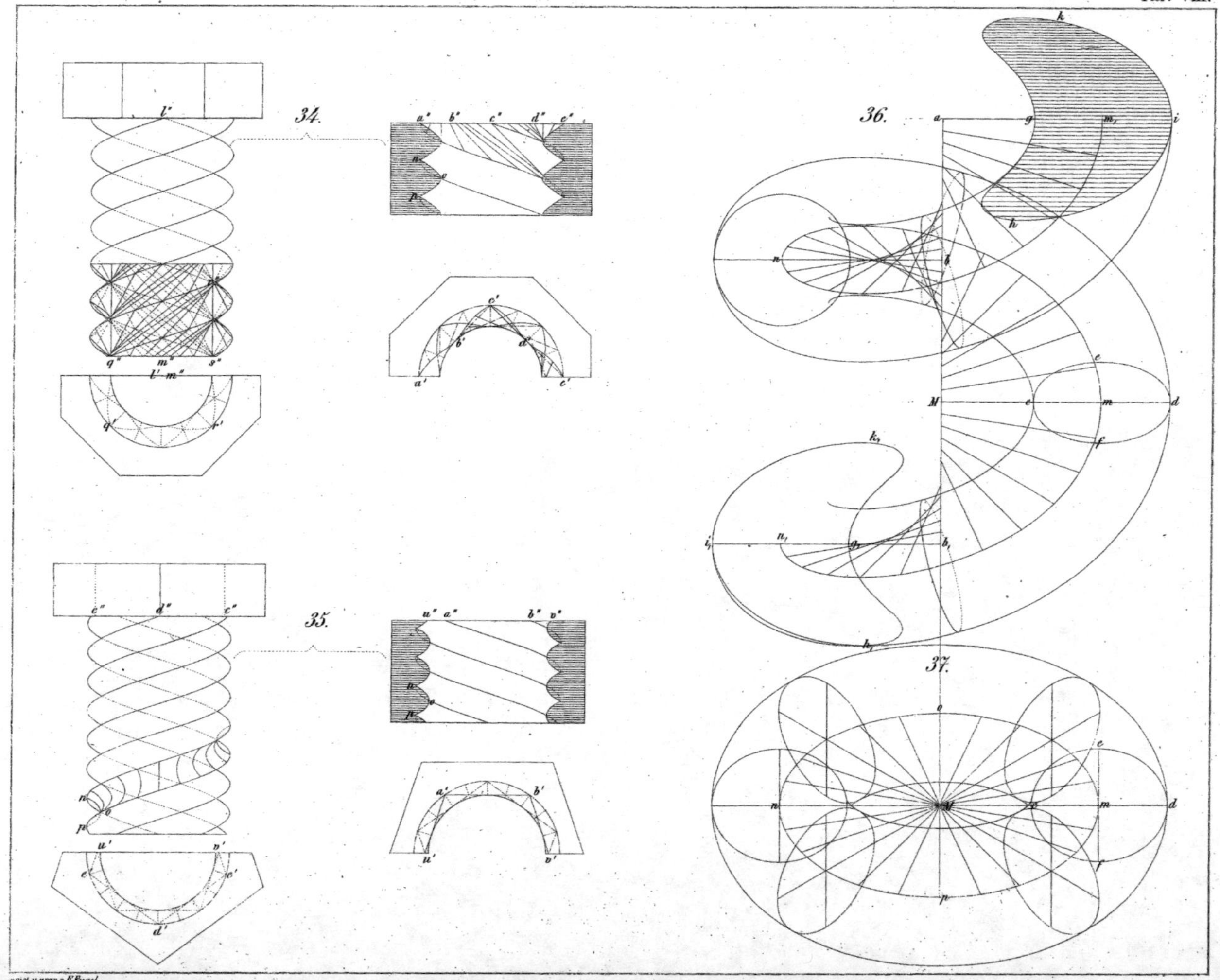
34.
35.
36.
37.

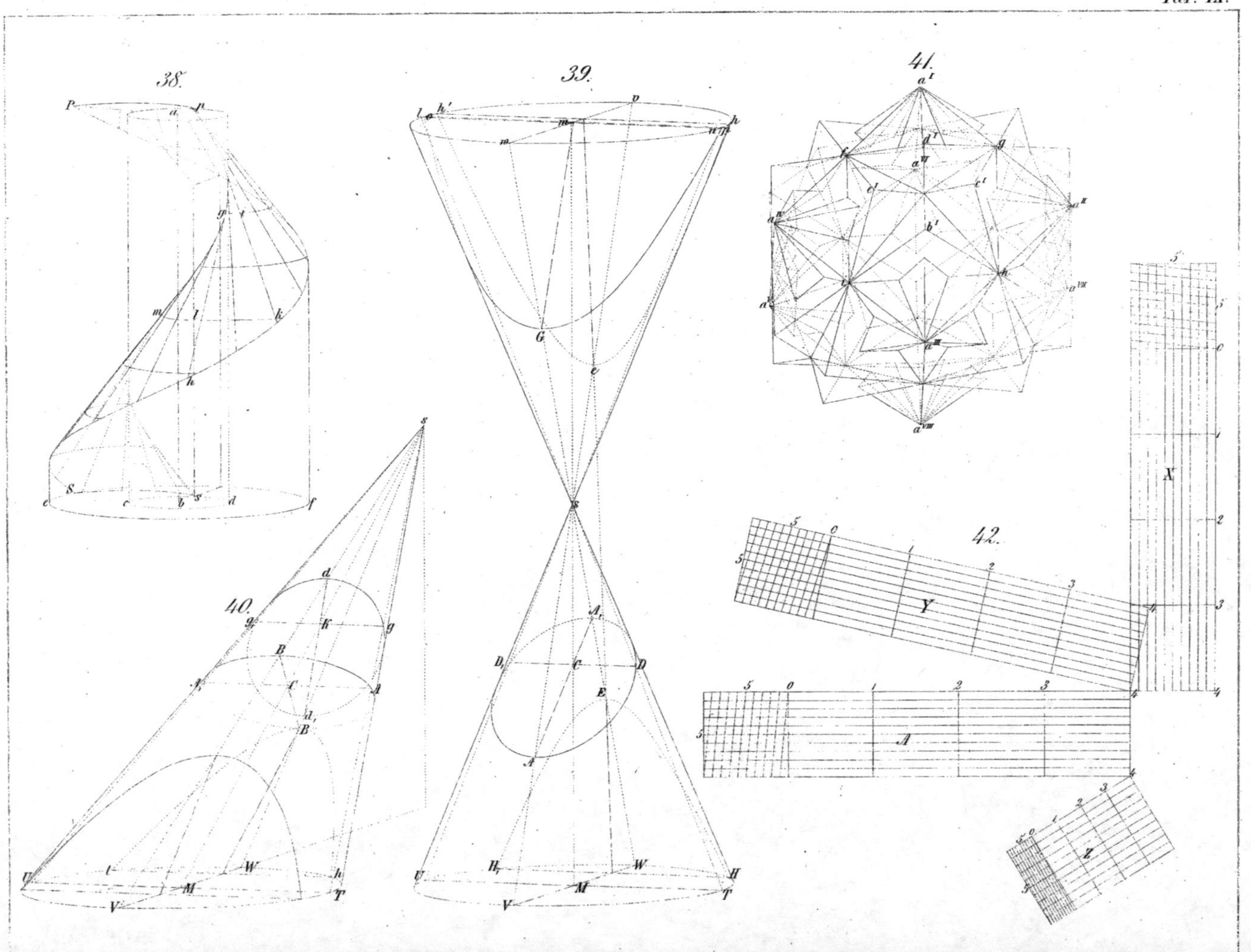
38.
39.
40.
41.
42.
Y
X
A
Z

EXPLANATIONS.

Towards the end of these explanations, some details will be entered into, respecting the particular projection—the axonometrical projection of some German authors—which has been made use of for the drawings.

1. Fresnel's wave surface in biaxial crystals.

(Plate II, fig. 9.)

Draw through the centre O of a triaxial ellipsoid any plane whatever, E, which will intersect the surface in an ellipse; erect in O a perpendicular to E, take on either side of O the lengths of the semi-axes of the ellipse; the resulting four points will be four points of the wave-surface. Giving all possible directions to the transversal plane E, you obtain the complete surface. It consists of two sheets, which correspond to the major and minor axes of the intersection-ellipses; and since among these ellipses there are only two with two equal axes—that is to say: which are circles—the two sheets will only have four points in common.

The wave surface has *three* principal sections, each of which consists of a circle and an ellipse. Suppose, to prove it, a system E_1, of planes drawn through an axis A of the ellipsoid; for all the ellipses, which will result, A will be the principal axis, whereas the second axis will be a diameter of the ellipsoid, perpendicular to A. Construct the points of the wave, which belong to all the planes E_1, and you will see, that they form a circle, the diameter of which is equal to the axis A, and an ellipse, the principal axes of which are equal to the two other axes of the ellipsoid. The circle will be exterior to the ellipse, if A be the greatest axis, it will be interior to the ellipse, if A be the least axis; and if A be the mean axis, the circle will intersect the ellipse at four points.

Fig. 9, Pl. II represents the wave-surface, the upper part on the right hand and the lower one at the left hand are withdrawn, to shew better the interior of the surface. The first principal section consists of a circle $A\,n\,A_1 n_1$ which incloses the ellipse $B\,s\,B_1 s_1$. The second principal section consists of an ellipse $A\,r\,A_1 r_1$ which incloses the circle $s\,C s_1\,C_1$. The third principal section consists of an ellipse $n\,C n_1\,C_1$, and of a circle $B\,r\,B_1 r_1$, the diameter of which is equal to the mean axis of the ellipsoid. These two curves meet in four points, two of which are denoted by P and P_1. While the tangents drawn through a point of a surface are in general situated in one single plane the tangent-plane, they form for the points P a cone of the second order. The discovery of these singular points of the surface is due to Sir William Hamilton of Dublin. The straight line PP_1, and a second straight line symmetrically situated with respect to the former are called secondary optical axes.—Two sections have been drawn through these axes and through the axis $s\,s_1$, which are indicated in the figure. The points T and Q are the points of contact of one of the four tangents common to the circle and the ellipse, the point T belongs to the circle. The plane drawn through $T\,Q$ perpendicular to the principal section, touches the surface along a circle of which $T\,Q$ is a diameter. The figure shows these four circles of contact, the straight line $O\,T$ is one of the two optical axes.

2. Figure 11 represents the Body inclosed by the interior sheet.

We will add, that PB, P_1B_1 are arcs of a circle, and that PC, P_1C_1 are elliptical arcs.

3. Triaxial Ellipsoid with two circular sections.

(Fig. 7 and 8, Pl. II.)

Fig. 7 represents the triaxial ellipsoid which has been made use of in the construction of the wave-surface: the axes are to each other in the proportion $\sqrt{3} : \sqrt{2} : 1$. Two diameters, KK_1 and kk_1 of the ellipse $A\,C\,A_1\,C_1$ are equal to the mean axis BB_1, it follows, that the sections containing the mean axis and one of these two diameters, are circles; the only ones the planes of which pass through the centre of the surface. It is known, that every section parallel to one of these two central sections is a circle.

Fig. 8 represents an ellipsoid divided into two halves by a circular section.

For the better understanding of the following we add these remarks: The name: "Line of curvature of a Surface" is given to a curved line along which the normals of the surface form a developable surface. Every surface has two systems of lines of curvature which intersect each other at right angles. Among all the plane sections drawn through a normal to the surface, those which contain the tangents to the lines of curvature, have the greatest or the least curvature, giving for the concavo-convex surfaces, a different sign to the curvature of the sections, which are in a different position to the tangent plane. The points of the surface, where all the normal sections have the same curvature are called: its *umbilici*. For the theory of the lines of curvature we are indebted to Monge.

4. Ellipsoid with its lines of curvature.

(Fig. 14, Pl. III.)

Figure 14 represents the two systems of the lines of curvature of the ellipsoid; the curve $d\,e\,f\,g$, for instance, belongs to the first system, the curve $o\,q\,p\,r$ to the other. The principal sections $A\,B\,A_1 B_1$ and $B\,C\,B_1\,C_1$, drawn through the mean axis, belong to different systems. As for the third section $A\,C\,A_1\,C_1$, two of its arcs, $n''n'$ and $n_{11}n_1$, are the limit-curves of the second system. The four points $n'\,n_1$, $n''n_{11}$ are the umbilici of the ellipsoid. The tangent-planes of the surface in these points are parallel to the two systems of circular sections; the circular section $k_1 B\ k\ B_1$ has been traced.

The lines of curvature of an ellipsoid can be constructed by the help of these four points, for—according to a most remarkable theorem due to Mr. Michael Roberts of Dublin—they bear with respect to the lines of curvature, a part analogous to that of the foci with respect to an ellipse; i. e.: if we fix the extremities of a thread to two umbilici which are not diametrically opposed, and stretch it by means of a style, thus bringing it close to the surface, the style, gliding over the surface, will describe one of its lines of curvature; but this is not the way by which the author determined them. He has found that in every quadrilateral formed by two couples of lines of curvature, the rectilinear diagonals are equal to each other. With the aid of this proposition, which subsists not only for the surfaces of the second order but also for the developable helicoid, he began by determining the vertices of a series of lines of curvature. One may consider, indeed, the figure $Cn'ef$ as a quadrilateral formed by two couples of lines of curvature; although two contiguous sides Cn' and $n'e$ are in one single plane. It follows: that $Ce = fn'$ (these distances being measured in a straight line); therefore, after having arbitrarily determined a vertex f on the principal section $B\,C\,B_1\,C_1$, the other vertex e will be found by the relation just indicated. The four vertices $f\,e\,d\,g$ determine the ellipse—projection of the curve $d\,e\,f\,g$ on the section $A_1B_1A\,B$—and the arc of the hyperbola—projection of the same curve on $B\,C\,B_1\,C_1$. After having constructed these two projections we shall be able to determine on the ellipsoid as many points of the lines of curvature as we please. For the curves of the second system we make use of the curves already drawn of the first system, and of the principal section $C\,B\,C_1B_1$ which belongs to the second system; for taking arbitrarily any point whatever of the principal section $A_1\,C\,A\,C_1$ as the vertex of a curve of the second system, it is obvious that one can determine, by the aid of our theorem, all its intersections with the curves of the first system. It is to avoid repetition, that we have entered on some details on this subject. We remark that in the hyperboloid of one sheet, and in the hyperbolical paraboloid, the existence of the generating straight lines allows of simplifications which the reader will find without difficulty.

5. Hyperboloid of two sheets.

(Fig. 12, Pl. III.)

This surface consists of two infinite and equal sheets, separated from one another. Suppose two hyperbolas having the same vertices and the planes of which are perpendicular to each other; an ellipse with variable axes, situated in a plane perpendicular to those of the two hyperbolas and the vertices of which are situated in these curves, generates the surface in question;—$A\,B\,A_1B_1$ is one of the positions of the variable ellipse. The right lines $a\,S\,a_1$, $b\,S\,b_1$ are the asymptotes to the two hyperbolas. An ellipsis described on $a\,a_1$, $b\,b_1$ as axes, determines with the vertex S a cone which is asymptote to the surface. The points $n\,n_1$ are the umbilici; a section drawn through $n\,o_1$—$n\,p\,o_1\,q$—parallel to the tangent plane in n_1 is a circle; both these circular sections have been traced in the figure. The dimensions of the hyperbola $A\,Z\,A_1$ are: $S\,Z = 18.2$, distance of the foci $= 47.4$, those of the ellipsis $A\,M = 61.3$, $BM = 40.7$. (Unit $= 1$ millimeter.)

6. The same surface with its lines of curvature.

(Fig. 13, Pl. III.)

7. Hyperboloid of one sheet and two circular sections of it.

(Fig. 25, Pl. VI.)

The surface is infinite but continuous. Same mode of generating as for the hyperboloid of two sheets, i. e.: by a movable ellipse, with this difference only, that it is the imaginary axis which is common to the directing hyperbolas. In that hyperbola in which the real axis is the minor one, there exist two diameters equal to the real axis AA_1 of the other; it follows, that you can draw through these diameters and through $A\,A'$ two circular sections $A\,o\,A_1n_1$ and $A\,o\,A_1n_1$. Through every point of the surface you can draw two right lines which lie altogether in the surface, as $f\,B\,g_1$ and $f'\,B\,g$. Every couple of right lines divides the surface into four regions, so that a plain section drawn through the point of the surface in question is a hyperbola or an ellipse, according to its situation in one or the other couple of these regions. The plane which contains all the tangents drawn through a point of the surface, passes also through those two right lines which cross each other there, and cuts the surface as well as it touches it.

8. Same surface with its lines of curvature.

(Fig. 26, Pl. III.)

The model and the diagram present besides the lines of curvature a great number of couples of generating right lines. It will easily be remarked that these right lines form two systems, thus, that the right lines of one system intersect all the right lines of the other system, whereas the right lines of one single system have no point in common. The tangents to the lines of curvature divide the angles between the generating right lines into equal parts.

Semi-axes of the hyperbola $fA_1a_1 = 24$; Semi-distance of the two foci $= 31$; Semi-axes of the elliptical minimum-section $= 24$ and $17{,}9$. (Unit $= 1$ millimeter.)

9. Elliptical paraboloid with two circular sections.

(Fig. 23, Pl. V.)

The generation of the surface by a movable ellipse is analogous to that of the hyperboloid, but the directing curves here are two parabolas having the same vertex and the same axis; $A\,B\,A_1B_1$ is one position of the ellipse.

The two points n and n_1 are umbilici; every section parallel to the planes tangent in n and n_1 is a circle.—We see in the figure the circles each of which passes through an umbilicus.

10. Same surface with its lines of curvature.

(Fig 24, Pl. V.)

The parameter of the parabola $A_1\,Z\,A$ stands to the axes of the ellipse $A_1\,B_1\,A\,B$ in the proportion of $25:61:43$.

11. Hyperbolical paraboloid; Oblique plane.

(Fig. 15, Pl. IV.)

Suppose two parabolas $Z'\,Z\,Z_1$ and $S_1\,Z\,S$ situated in two planes perpendicular to each other and in such a position that their vertices coincide and that the axis of one of them is the prolongation of the axis of the other.—If one of these two curves— $S_1\,Z\,S$ for instance—moves in such a manner, that its plane remains parallel to its first position, and that its vertex Z goes along the other curve, it will describe a hyperbolical paraboloid. Of all the surfaces we have yet examined this is the only one the plane sections of which are never closed curves, i. e. ellipses.

Like the hyperboloid of one sheet it has the property of having every point passed through by two right lines lying altogether in the surface; the right lines of each of the two systems (see No. 8) are parallel to one plane. Thence follows a second way of generation for the paraboloid: It is generated by a right line which, always remaining parallel to a plane, rests upon two oblique right lines; a property which gave to this paraboloid the name of "Oblique plane".

12. Same surface with its lines of curvature.

(Fig. 16, Pl. IV.)

The tangents of the lines of curvature are the bisectors of the angles between the right lines of the surface.

The proportion of the parameters of the two parabolas is 25,6 : 10.

13. Right elliptical cone with two circular sections.

(Fig. 4, Pl. I)

All the circular sections as $hfig$ and $hdie$ are perpendicular to the plane drawn through the vertex and the minor axis BB_1 of the basis.

14. Same surface with its lines of curvature.

(Fig. 5, Pl. I)

The sides of the surface are the first system of lines of curvature, the curves of the second system are the intersections of the cone with concentric spheres described round the vertex S of the cone as their center.

15. Double right circular cone with three sections.

(Fig. 39, Pl. IX.)

The curve A_1D_1AD is an ellipse, uGt is a parabola, $hek'HEH_1$ a hyperbola.

16. Oblique circular-based cone with four sections.

(Fig. 40, Pl. IX.)

The section A_1BAB_1 is an ellipse, the angle A_1SA is the greatest of all the angles formed by two sides of the cone: gdg_1d_1 is the circumference of a circle the plane of which is not parallel to the base (see No. 13); tBh is a hyperbola, and the section parallel to the side sW which is not marked with letters is a parabola.

17. Combination of a sphere and a right elliptical cone.

(Fig. 3, Pl. I.)

We have given one horizontal projection and two vertical ones.

The ellipse $ABCD$ is the base of the cone. Round the point m'' in the axis of the cone a sphere has been described which touches the two sides drawn from the vertex of the surface to the extremities of the basis. Their projection on the first vertical plane is the ellipse $n''c''d''$, on the second vertical plane drawn through the axis CD their projections are two right lines, whereas their horizontal projections are two ellipses.

We find by a similar method the circular sections in the other surfaces of the second order.

18. Body inclosed between two squares and four oblique planes.

(Fig. 20, Pl. V.)

In a right prism with a square base the diagonals of the lateral faces have been drawn. A right line AB which—always remaining parallel to the base—moves along two of these diagonals Aa, Bb will describe a part of a hyperbolical paraboloid, i. e. of an oblique plan.

The same construction is to be used for the three other faces. Every section parallel to the base is a square; the smallest section is that which passes through the center of the body.

19. Body inclosed between one square and four oblique planes.

(Fig. 18, Pl. IV.)

The right line EF is a parallel to the diagonal AC of the square $ABCD$, the right lines EA, FC are perpendicular to the plane of the square. G, the middle of EF, has been joined to the points D and B by two right lines which form with EA and FC the directrices of four oblique planes, the generatrices of which remain constantly parallel to the basis. Every horizontal section is a parallelogramm with four equal sides.

20. Parallelopiped divided by an oblique plane into two unequal parts.

(Fig. 19, Pl. IV.)

The oblique plane passes from the edge ad to the diagonal AC of the opposite face.

The name of "Helix" is given to a curve situated on a circular-based right cylinder, the vertical ordinates of which are proportional to the arcs of the base, these are measured from the point, where the Helix meets the basis. The height to which the helix has risen after one full revolution is the path of the helix.

21. Right Helicoid.

(Fig. 30, Pl. VII.)

The surface is generated by the motion of a right line which, remaining parallel to the circular base of a right cylinder, passes through its axis and is supported by a helix which is traced on the surface of the cylinder. The curve $a\,1\,2\,3\,4\,5\,6\,7\,b$ is the curve of contact of a cylinder, circumscribed to the helicoid, it is a second helix the path of which is half the path of the first one.—It is traced on a second cylinder which contains the axis of the given cylinder. The horizontal section of the circumscribed cylinder is a cycloid the generating circle of which is equal to the base of the second cylinder.

The surface being infinite, the diagram represents only that part of it which is comprised between two planes perpendicular to the axis and a right cylinder concentric to the first one. Same observation for the following surfaces.

22. Oblique Helicoid.

(Fig. 31, Pl. VII.)

It differs from the preceding surface inasmuch, as the movable right line forms with the axis a constant angle which is not a right one. The curve $c'd'a'g'v'$ is the intersection of the surface with the superior horizontal plane.

23. General Helicoid.

(Fig. 32, Pl. VII.)

It is described by a right line of constant inclination towards the basis of the cylinder and of constant distance from the axis, while one of its points, the extremity of the shortest distance, describes a helix. The horizontal projections of all the generating right lines touch a circle, the base of the cylinder on which the helix is situated. The curve $c' d' v'$ is a horizontal section of the surface; $v'' p'' o'' n''$ is a vertical section drawn through the axis.

24. Developable Helicoid.

(Fig. 33, Pl. VII.)

A ruled surface is said to be developable if two generating right lines, infinitely near to one another, are situated in one plane, which allows of extending its parts on a plane without any tearing or creasing. The most simple developable surfaces are the cylinders and cones in which the generators are parallel or convergent. In all other developable surfaces the right lines are tangents to a curve of double curvature called the edge of regression. The developable helicoid is the locus of the tangents to a helix the vertical projection of which is seen in $t'' o'' c''$. The curve $c' d' g' v'$ (part of the involute of a circle) is a horizontal section, the curve $m'' p'' o'' n''$ belongs to a vertical section drawn through the axis.

25. Same surface with its lines of curvature.

(Fig. 38, Pl. IX.)

We have represented only the inferior half of the surface. The generating right lines are one of the two systems of lines of curvature (which they are in all developable surfaces) the other system are plain sections perpendicular to the axis.

26. Screw of four grooves with its nut.

(Fig. 34, Pl. VIII.)

A screw is said to have two, three, four grooves, if one, two, three other grooves have been inserted between two consecutive turns of the thread. The surface of these grooves of the screw is shaped in the diagram, No. 26, according to the general helicoid.

27. Screw of five grooves with its nut.

(Fig. 35, Pl. VIII.)

Every section perpendicular to the axis is a regular pentagon; the screw is generated by the motion of this pentagon, the five vertices of which describe five helices situated on the same cylinder.

28. Oblique surface.

(Fig. 21, Pl. V.)

Suppose $a\,b$, A B to be two right lines of equal length which do not meet, and the angle between their directions to be a right one as well as the angles between $a\,b$, A B and the right line $m\,M$ which joins their centers. Describe on these two lines $a\,b$ and A B two semi-circumferences, divide them into equal parts, and from these points of division draw perpendiculars to $a\,b$ and A B. We in this way get, on each of these lines, a series of points unequally distant from one another. The surface represented by No. 21 will be described by a straight line joining at first the middle M and the extremity b and meeting then successively every two points of division of the two right lines; $b\,M$ and m A are two of its positions. It is very easily seen that it passes twice over $a\,b$ and A B. Every plane section perpendicular to the axis $M m$ is an ellipse the vertices of which lie in the triangles A m B and $a\,M\,b$. The mean section is the circumference of a circle.

29. Oblique surface; elliptical wedge.

(Fig. 22, Pl. V.)

The straight line $a\,a_1$ is equal and parallel to the axis $B\,B_1$ of the ellipse $A_1 B_1\,AB$; and aB, $a_1 B_1$ are perpendicular to the plane of the ellipse. A movable straight line supported by the ellipse, always remaining parallel to the plane $m\,A\,A_1$, will describe the surface in question. Every plain section perpendicular to the axis $m\,M$ is an ellipse. If $A\,A_1$ is greater than $B\,B_1$ one of these sections will be a circle.

30. Oblique plane; semicircular wedge.

(Fig. 17, Pl. IV.)

The base is a semicircle; otherwise the same generation as for No. 29.

31. Developable surface.

(Fig. 28, Pl. VI.)

A circular right cylinder of which $M\,a\,u$ is half the base meets a sphere discribed with the radius $M\,a$ round the center so that one of its sides passes through the centre of the sphere. Their intersection is a curve of double curvature of which $p\,t\,a$ is a part. The developable surface represented by fig. 28, is the locus of the tangents to this curve. The figure shows the two sheets of the surface; the lower sheet is rendered visible, the upper one being limited by the vertical plane $b\,c\,a$.

32. Developable surface.

(Fig. 29, Pl. VI.)

The surface represented by fig. 29 is the locus of the tangents to the curve $sS_1\,s_1 S$ which is the intersection of two right cylinders. The base of one of them is the circle AA_1 in the horizontal plane, and half the base of the other is the semi-circumference $s\,Z\,s$, in the vertical plane. The figure represents a part of the two sheets contained between four vertical and one horizontal plane. The curves $h\,b\,u$ and $r\,b\,f$ are the intersections of the two sheets with one of the vertical planes; the curve $o\,l$—the prolongation of which has been dotted—is the intersection of a horizontal plane; so it is with the curve $n\,k$.

33. Serpentine body.

(Fig. 36, Pl. VIII. Isometrical projection.)

This body is generated by the motion of a circle, the plane of which remains perpendicular to a helix while its centre describes the latter curve. To construct the outline of the body spheres have been described round several points of the helix with a radius equal to that of the generating circle. The envelope of the outline of these spheres gives the out-

required. The figure exhibits several ellipses which are projections of the generating circle; the straight lines belong to a right helicoid.

34. Annular body.

(Fig. 37, Pl. VIII. Isometrical projection.)

This body is generated by the motion of a circle the center of which describes a second circle, while its plane remains perpendicular to the directing circle. The construction of the outline has been performed on the same principles as that of the preceding body. Several positions of the generating circle have been indicated.

35. Spherical curve with its polar curve.

(Fig. 27, Pl. VI.)

This spherical curve is the intersection of a sphere and of two right cylinders. The bases of these cylinders have a diameter equal to the radius of the sphere; they touch each other and the equator of the sphere, in the plane of which they are described. In fig. 27 these two bases are seen in the horizontal plane; the vertical projection of the intersecting curve is $p'' d'' b''$.

Suppose a system of planes drawn through the centre of the sphere and through the tangents to the spherical curve and erect diameters perpendicular to these planes: the intersecting curve of the spherical surface formed by these diameters is the polar curve to the given curve. We have constructed the horizontal and the vertical projection of this polar curve.

36. Sphere with four great circles.

(Fig. 6, Pl. I.)

Through the diameter Pp have been drawn three great circles of the sphere, the great circle $A\ B\ C\ D$ is perpendicular to the diameter Pp.

37. Spherical triangle with its symmetrical and polar triangle.

(Fig. 10, Pl. II.)

Three diameters of a sphere $A'' A_{11}$, $B'' B_{11}$, $C'' C_{11}$ determine the vertices of two symmetrical triangles $A''\ B''\ C''$, $B_{11}\ B_{11}\ C_{11}$. The three great circles the planes of which are perpendicular to the three diameters determine eight triangles. The angles and sides of two of these triangles are the supplements of the sides and angles of the given triangle; or—which comes to the same—of the symmetrical triangle. These two triangles are called the polar triangles of the given triangle. The figure shows only one of them: $D_{11}\ E_{11}\ F_{11}$.

38. Combination of five cubes.

(Fig. 41, Pl. IX.)

The cube $a^{I}\ a^{II}\ a^{III}\ a^{IV}\ a^{V}\ a^{VI}\ a^{VII}\ a^{VIII}$ is pierced by four other cubes B, C, D, E. Each of its four diagonals coincides with a diagonal of B, C, D and E. The lines of intersection of the faces of the first cube and of those of the four others form with the edges of the first two species of angles; those of the first species are equal to 45°, and those of the other are = 26° 33′, 9 i. e. = arc (tang-= 0,5).

Most of the bodies of which our collection contains the models have three axes perpendicular to one another. To make the understanding of the diagrams which represent them more easy, we may choose as plane of projection a vertical plane which is not parallel to any one of the axes. It is evident, that the lengths of a line parallel to an axis stand to their projections in a constant ratio which, generally, will be a different one for every other axis. If these three ratios are equal, the position of the axes in respect to the plane of projection is the same as that of three convergent edges of a cube in respect to the plane perpendicular to the diagonal which passes through the vertex formed by the edges. To this special projection the name of *isometrical* projection has been given (see fig. 36 and 37) and to the general projection that of *axonometrical* projection.

Suppose (fig. 1, pl. I) $y'\ o'\ (z')\ c$ the base of cube situated in the horizontal plane, turn this face about $o'\ o''$ downwards, till the perpendicular distance from the point c to the horizontal plane be equal to $a\ d$, and determine the projection of the cube and especially of the three edges drawn through o' (which may be considered as three axes of orthogonal coordinates) on a vertical plane drawn through $o'\ o''$. To give more clearness to the figure, we have constructed this projection in O—to the right, above—so that $o''\ o'$ forms a part of the horizon $o''\ y''\ z''\ a$. The vertical edge drawn through o' will remain perpendicular to the horizon in O, but it will be shortened. Draw through d a parallel to $o''\ a$ and describe with $o''\ a$ an arc of a circle about o'', join their intersection and the point o'' by a right line: the angle $a\ o''\ (z)$ will be the measure of the revolution of the cube. Erect in o'' on $o''\ (z)$ a perpendicular $o''\ (x_1)$ equal to the edge $o''\ x''$: the angle $x''\ o''\ (x_1)$, evidently, will be equal to the aforesaid angle. Erect in O a perpendicular to the horizon, draw through (x) a parallel to the latter line, and we shall obtain the projection of the vertical edge of the cube.— To determine the projection of the horizontal edge $o'\ y'$ take on the horizon, at the right side from O a length equal to $o'\ o''$, erect at its extremity a perpendicular to the horizon which goes downwards, make—on $o''\ (z)$—$o''\ (y)$ equal to $o''\ y''$, draw through (y) a parallel to the horizon which meets the last mentioned perpendicular in y, and $O\ y$ will be the projection of the edge $o''\ y'$. Same construction for the second horizontal edge $o''\ z'$ the projection of which is $O\ z$.

If the edge of the cube is the unit of length, the three right lines $o\ x$, $o\ y$, $o\ z$ may serve as units of length for the projections of the straight lines parallel to the axes.

We will solve now the inverse problem:

The units of length L, M, N being given for the projections of the straight lines parallel to the three axes, find the angles between the projections of the axes:

Suppose r to be the unit of length (the edge of the cube) α, β, γ to be the angles between the plane of projection and the axes (three convergent edges of the cube): then you will obtain:

$L = r \cos \alpha$, $M = r \cos \beta$, $N = r \cos \gamma$,

whence

$$L^2 + M^2 + N^2 = r^2 (\cos \alpha^2 + \cos \beta^2 + \cos \gamma^2)$$

but

$$\cos \alpha^2 + \cos \beta^2 + \cos \gamma^2 = 2$$

thus

$$r = \sqrt{\tfrac{1}{2} (L^2 + M^2 + N^2)}$$

a formula which allows of a very simple construction. We have executed this construction supposing: $L = 1$, $M = \frac{23}{24}$, $N = \frac{8}{24}$ (see fig. 2, pl. I.) These same numbers are adopted too for the scales (fig. 42, pl. IX). The scale designated by A refers to the unity of length, while X, Y, Z are scales of reduction for the three axes. To come back to our problem: Decribe with the radius r a circle about m, take on the radius $m n$ the lengths $m x' = L$, $m y' = M$, $m z' = N$, erect the perpendiculars $x' p$, $y' q$, $z' s$: then the angles $p m x'$, $q m y'$, $s m z'$ will be equal to the inclinations α, β, γ.

These being found, the problem of determining the angles between the projections of the axes, the units of the scales of reduction being given, is to be solved in the following manner: Suppose through *p—that* extremity of the edge of the cube which is the nearer one to the plane of projection —a plane parallel to the latter. It is obvious, that this new plane will determine on the second axis a segment equal to $m v$. The rectangular triangle between the first axis and the segment of the second one, will have for its projection a second triangle one side of which is equal to the known hypotenuse of the triangle in space, while the two other sides are equal to $m x'$ and to the projection of $m v$ on $m n$, i. e. to $m' v$.

With the help of these three right lines the triangle $X O v'$ (fig. 2*b*) has been constructed in which the angle in O is the angle between the projections of the two axes. The position of the projection of the third axis will be found by drawing $O Z$ perpendicular to $X v'$. Indeed, the third axis being perpendicular to the plane of the projected triangle, its projection must be perpendicular to the trace of this plane; but $X v'$ is parallel to this trace; $O Z$, therefore, must be perpendicular to $X v'$.

The problem we have just solved is a special case of another well known problem, viz of the reduction of an angle to the horizon.

TESTIMONIALS.

I have great pleasure in offering my testimony to the extraordinary beauty and value of Mr. Engel's Collection of Geometrical and Optical Models. It is not always easy for a student to obtain clear and accurate conceptions of the relations of space from diagrams alone, and there are probably few teachers who have not often felt the want of a complete and well executed series of models. Mr. Engel's beautiful collection will be found to be a most desirable addition to the usual method of instruction in Geometry and Optics, and I earnestly recommend it to the attention of teachers and students.

WOLCOTT GIBBS,

Prof. Chemistry and Physics in the Free Academy in New York. June 26th, 1855.

TWO LETTERS TO THE AUTHOR.

Beifolgend erlaube ich mir die mir gütigst mitgetheilten Zeichnungen nebst Text mit besonderem Danke zu remittiren. Ich weiss in der That nicht, ob ich Ihre "schönen Modelle" höher schätzen soll oder "die Zeichnungen," und glaube, dass beide in Verbindung mit einander beim Unterricht erst recht fruchtbar sein werden. Vollenden die erstern die dem Anfänger oft schwierige Vorstellung der Flächen und Linien, um die es sich handelt, so zeigen die letztern die graphische Darstellung in einer Vollkommenheit, die nichts zu wünschen übrig lässt und in vielen Fällen mehr leistet als die körperliche Construction.

Der Text ist zum Verständniss dessen, was gegeben ist, ausreichend. Für den Gebrauch, der in dem Bereich meiner Wirksamkeit von den Blättern gemacht werden wird, hätte ich an manchen Stellen ein Eingehen auf die Entstehungsweise der Figuren, eine Angabe der Constructionen gewünscht. Dadurch hätten die Blätter zugleich als eine Aufgaben-Sammlung gedient. Indessen verkenne ich nicht, dass die Arbeit, wie sie vorliegt, für das grössere Publikum besser passt. Ich wünsche, dass das letztere recht gross sein möge, und kann ich hierzu etwas beitragen, so wird es mir zum Vergnügen gereichen.

Berlin, 14. Juli 1854.

DRUCKENMÜLLER,

Director des Königl. Gewerbeinstitutes.

Mr. Engel de cette ville, duquel la rare perfection avec laquelle il exécute toute sorte de dessins géometriques et la précision vraiment surprenante avec laquelle il construit en relief les objets si variés sur lesquels s'exerce la haute Géometrie, ont valu depuis longtemps dans ce pays-ci la vive approbation de tous les professeurs qui ont été à même d'apprécier les grands secours que les dessins et les modèles de Mr. Engel fournissent à l'enseignement, étant sur le point de s'expatrier, je me plais à exprimer la haute estime que j'ai conçue pour son beau talent. Puisse son talent aussi rare qu'il est utile, avoir aussi ailleurs tout le succès qu'il mérite.

Berlin, le 7 Août 1854.

G. LEJEUNE DIRICHLET,

Membre de l'Académie de Berlin, associé de l'Institute de France.

www.ingramcontent.com/pod-product-compliance
Lightning Source LLC
LaVergne TN
LVHW011627120826
845150LV00012B/2351
* 9 7 8 1 4 1 8 1 9 3 5 7 7 *